EGG-CARTON ZOO

EGG-CARTON ZOO

Rudi Haas and Hans Blohm

———○———

with an introduction by
David Suzuki

Toronto
OXFORD UNIVERSITY PRESS

Produced by
Boulton Publishing Services Inc., Toronto
Designed by Fortunato Aglialoro

© Oxford University Press (Canadian Branch) 1986
OXFORD is a trademark of Oxford University Press

78 - 098
ISBN 19-540513-7

Printed in Hong Kong

Canadian Cataloguing in Publication Data
Haas, Rudi.
    Egg-carton zoo

ISBN 0-19-540513-7

1. Egg carton craft – Juvenile literature. 2. Animals
– Models – Juvenile literature. 3. Zoo animals –
Models – Juvenile literature. 4. Animals – Juvenile
literature. I. Blohm, Hans. II. Suzuki, David T.,
1936 –   III. Title.

TT870.H3 1986   j745.59′2   C86-093022-X

INTRODUCTION
by David T. Suzuki

Imagine being able to creep through a jungle and coming upon a muddy river-pool full of crocodiles, giant turtles and hippos. At the water's edge are birds, elephants, leopards and antelopes. Wouldn't you love to spend time in such a wonderful place? Well, you CAN and the greatest thing about this adventure is that the wonderful creatures who live here will all be made by YOU! That is the promise of this delightful book.

Rudi Haas, who has produced this book, is an artist with a magical touch. The first time he showed me some of his egg-carton animals, I was immediately enchanted. Somehow he has been able to capture a lifelike quality in his animals—the antelope seems nervous and ready to jump aside, the elephant prepares to defend its baby, the frog springs to safety. I wanted to take them home to my children right away. But even more than that—I wanted to make some *myself*. I went home and immediately made a huge mess in the kitchen and triumphantly managed a turtle. But I couldn't match Rudi's. I needed practice and I needed Rudi to help me. Well, now, with this book, I, and you, can do it. The book shows pictures of the completed animals and a clear way of making them.

Now remember, Rudi is a genius. He has a quality that few grownups still have, an openness and imagination that children possess. I am amazed at how he can 'see', through his imagination, the outlines of creatures struggling to get out of the bumps and valleys of an ordinary egg-carton. Try following his instructions. You'll feel clumsy at first but you'll get better and faster with practice. And then, you'll start coming up with variations of your *own*, even new ones that aren't in the book. It's easy to spend hours making egg-carton animals and playing with them. That's the essence of how we learn to see things around us and to invent new things. It's all *fun*, but as an added bonus, it has given us a way of *recycling* material instead of adding it to a heap of garbage.

So turn the page and begin your own adventure into the world of egg-carton animals.

DAVID T. SUZUKI

EGG-CARTON ZOO
by Rudi Haas

Egg-cartons are wonderfully shaped.

It's no coincidence that we can see the basic forms of creatures in these boxes, shaped and moulded as they are to hold and protect eggs.

Eggs contain all life-giving things....

So do these boxes for our 'look-alike' egg-carton creatures. Anybody who can recognize an animal by its shape, and is able to handle a pair of scissors, can 'hatch' some 'look-alikes' from these boxes.

I would like to share with you some of my experiences and observations. They might ease your way to your own discoveries.

Hold the box upside down!

You see the turtle shell?

Look at the inside of the cover!

You see the hump of a whale or the back of a horse?

You don't have to be able to draw any of the creatures on paper. Just use your imagination. All that's needed beside the styrofoam boxes is a pair of curved nail-scissors and a *big* spark of enthusiasm!

Let your eyes wander from shape to shape on the inside or outside of the box. Figures will emerge like magic. You will find that the secret of your success is partly due to the material itself. The shaped forms of the boxes let loose your imagination. They don't intimidate you like so many other more precious materials. Just start cutting!

If any of your creatures doesn't come up to your expectations you can blame it on the box and discard it. Only a protesting 'squigg' may be heard as you crunch the box into the garbage.

Sometimes, though, you will succeed with the first attempt, but with some figures it may take more than one try, over a period of time.

Start with simple shapes, like a turtle or a bird. Have fun and enjoy what you are doing.

There are no rules or regulations!

The main idea of this little book is to encourage you in your own experiments. They will lead on to endless, exciting new discoveries.

RUDI HAAS

Cutting out the shape

So now our chick has hatched and what is he going to become? He is going to grow into an Eagle!

You might think that because the eagle is such a kingly bird he will be difficult to make. Not so, the eagle is very simple, and oddly enough we find him in the same part of the egg-carton where later on we shall find the frog....

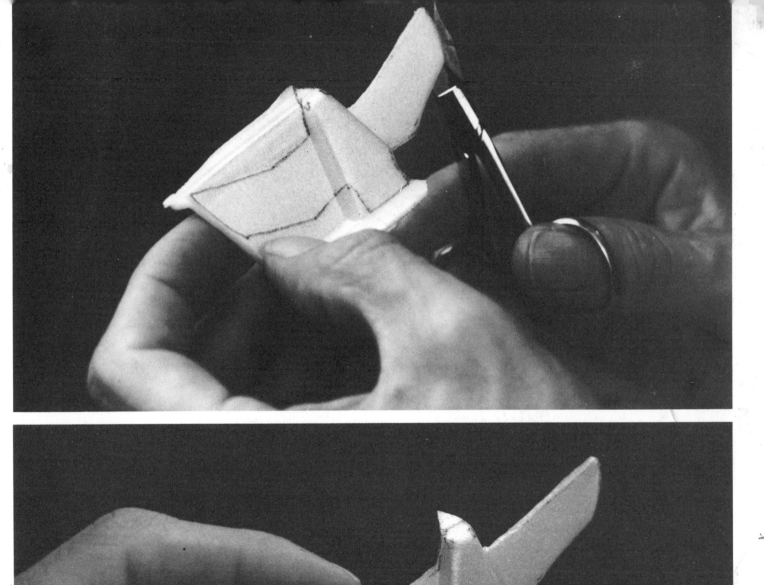

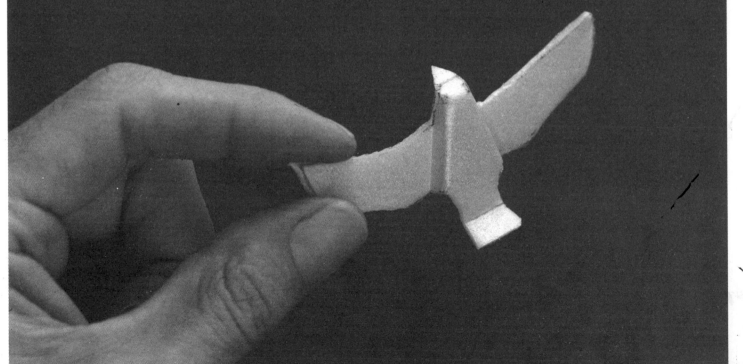

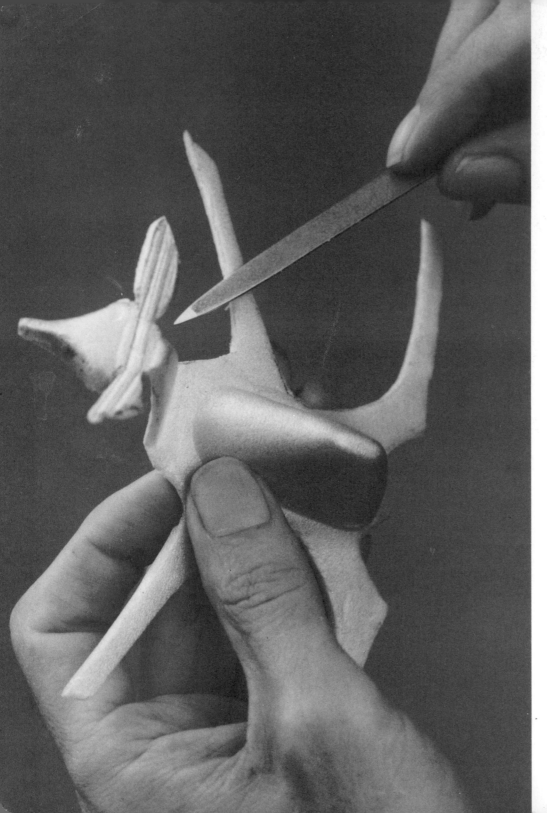

Finishing Touches

There are many ways to give the surface of these figures different textures by wrinkling, stamping or engraving it. You will no doubt discover some methods of your own. To change a shape, the material can be softened by repeated finger pressures (squizzes). Also by holding a cut figure with chopsticks into hot water or steam (not boiling water though; watch out!), so that it can be reshaped before it hardens again.

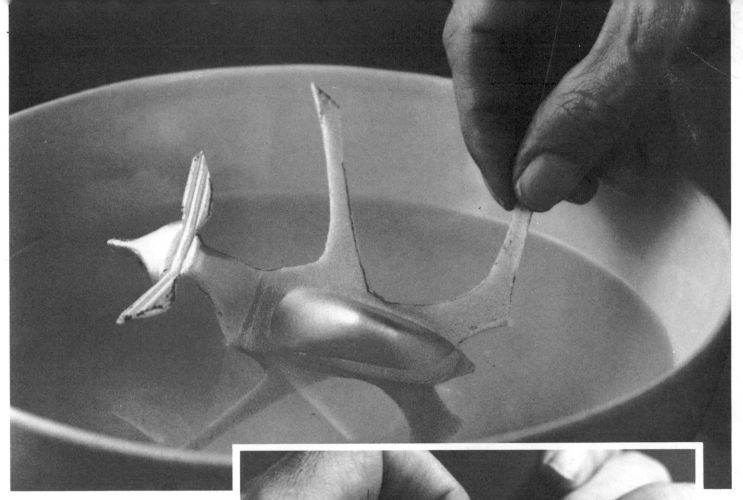

To colour a figure, many substances can be used. A few drops of hot water on instant-coffee powder or a pinch of spice (like saffron) can do wonders. Saffron for instance will give your figures a permanent, deep, golden metallic glow. As with all other water-soluble colourings you should mix in a few drops of detergent, so that the colour will stick to the waxy surface of the carton.

Frogs!

Frogs make us smile!

From the frog-eggs, first tadpoles develop, which swim under the water, then they change to frogs who can jump around.

Some species of frogs can climb trees, others live only on the ground. In the spring we often hear frog concerts.

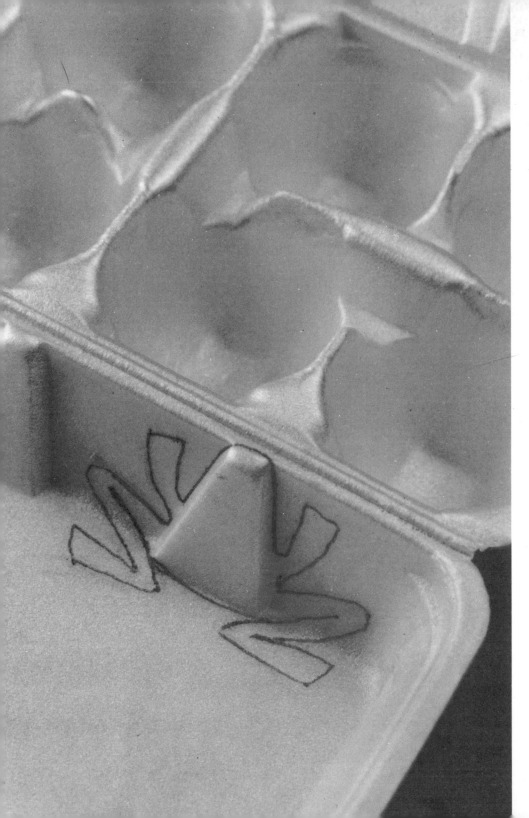

Here is a frog, hiding in the bottom of the egg carton. Now you will see how we cut him out and set him ready to jump. So turn the page....

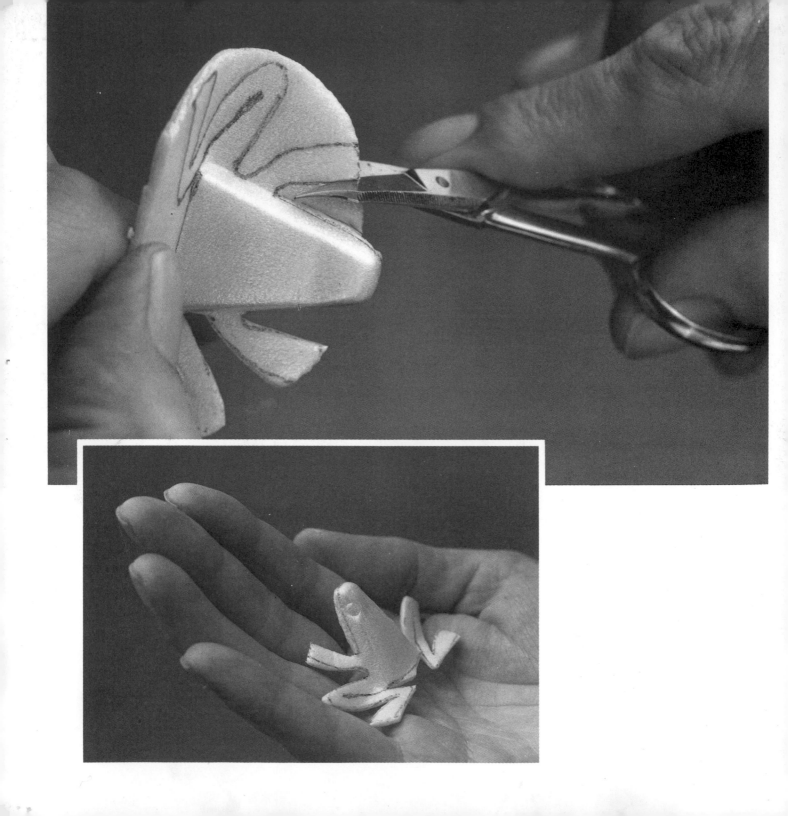

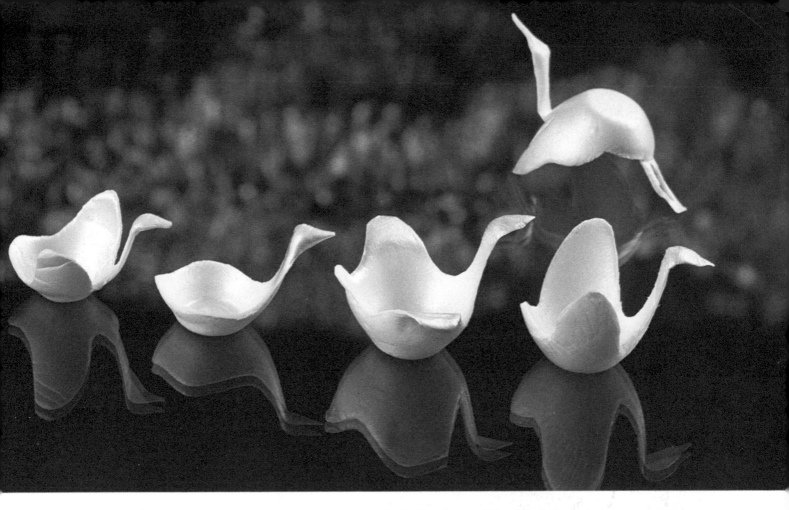

Waterbirds

Ducks, geese and swans have much in common with other waterbirds.

They can swim, fly, and walk on land. Once they are in the air they become good flyers.

They need a certain length of 'runway' to take off on water. When they 'land' on water they put on their brakes to stop fast.

They prefer clear water, where they can see their food better when they dip their long necks.

Some man-made chemicals in the water can dissolve the waxlike waterproof coating of their feathers. The birds need that coating to keep afloat and stay warm. If the coating is removed the birds can't 'take off' easily and what's more they can suffer from the cold.

Many of the waterbirds migrate between countries and even between continents from season to season. Their 'homeland' is where they are born. Canada geese spend more time abroad than at home. So do these birds belong to anywhere or nowhere?

When birds migrate they flock together and become a singing cloud, but not all such clouds sound musical to our human ears....

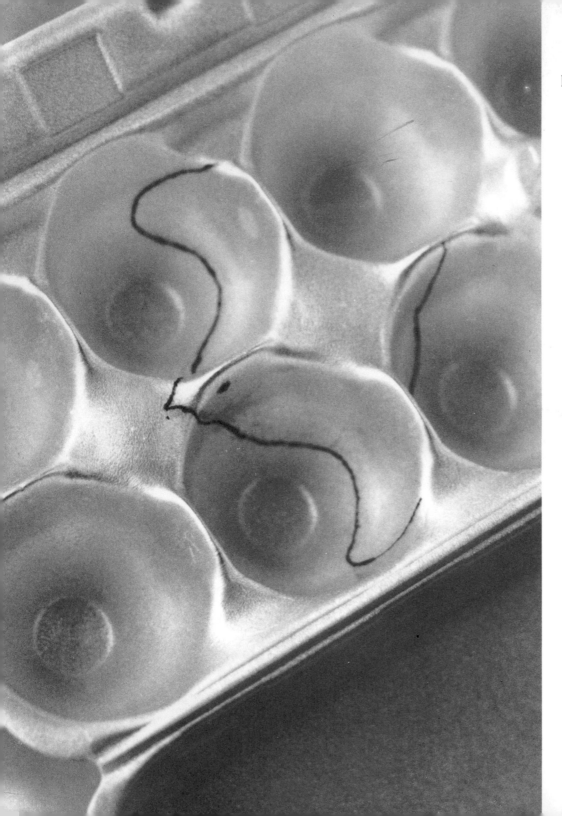

How to make a Bird...

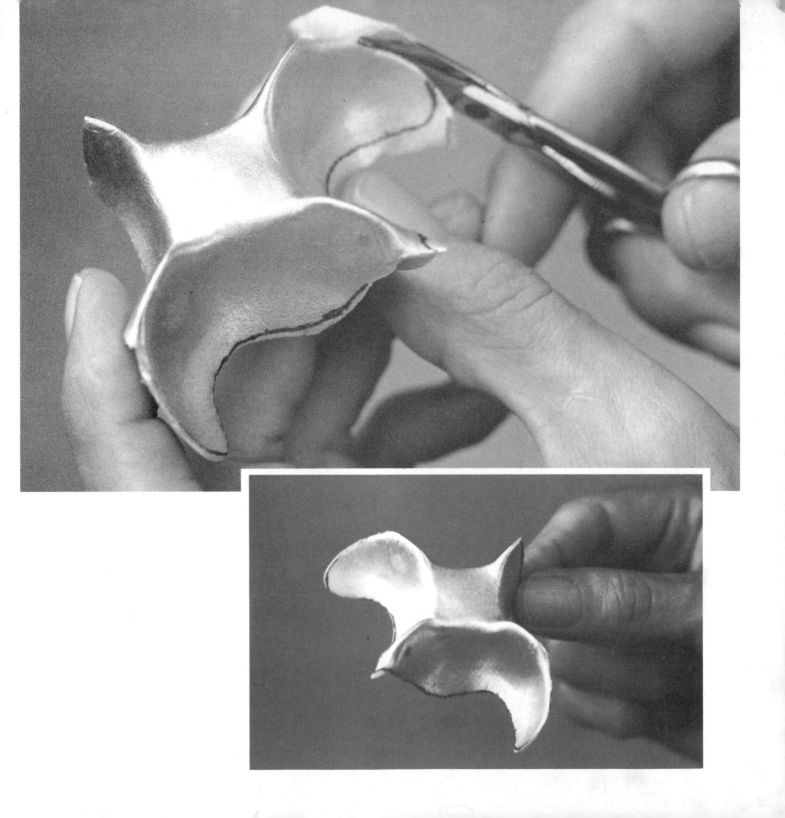

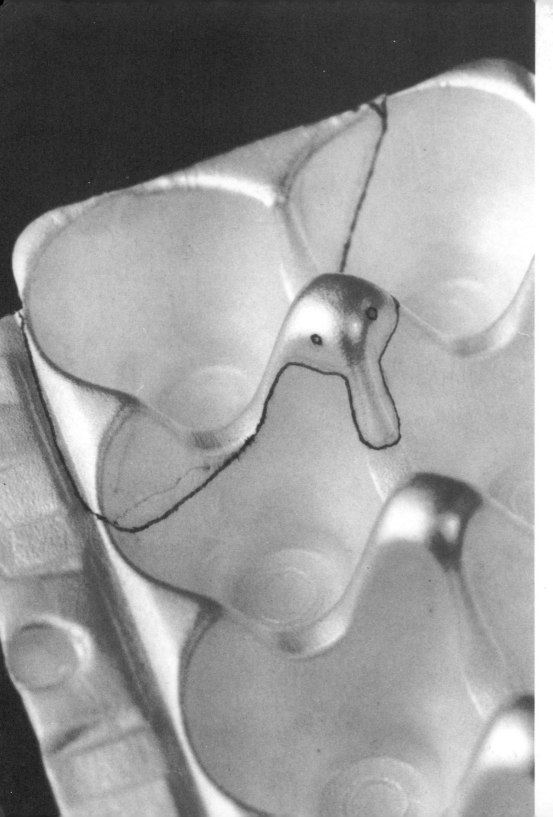

How to make a Duck...

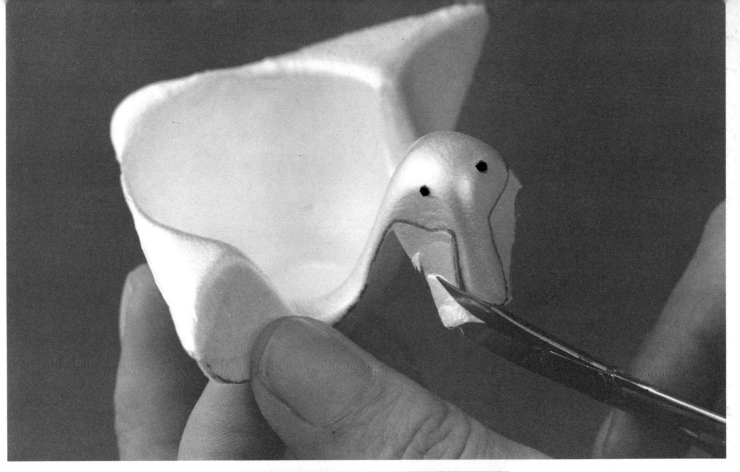

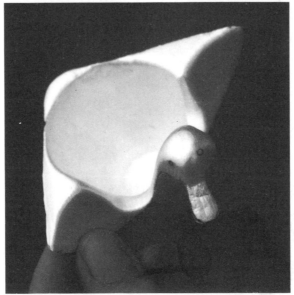

How to make a Swan...

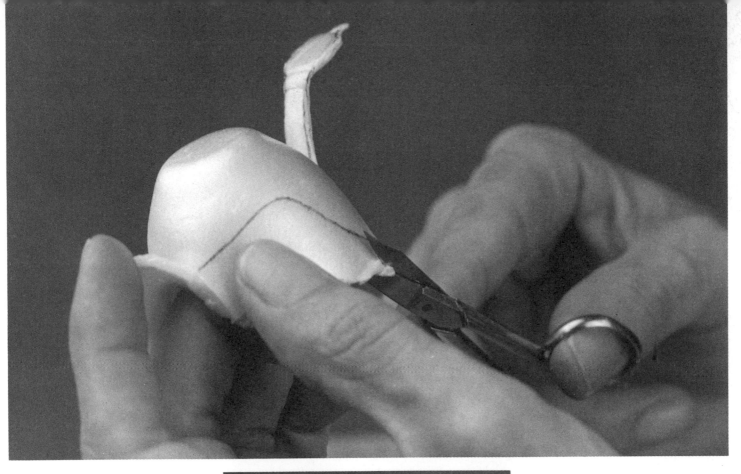

Pigs

Most pigs that we see on a farm are naked, pinkish in color and somewhat roundish in shape. They can be noisy at times but at least they're not fussy about their food!

The young piglets are curious and keep themselves busy turning things, even the earth, upside down. The greater the mess, the happier they seem to be. But then they never have to clean up afterwards....

How to make a Pig...

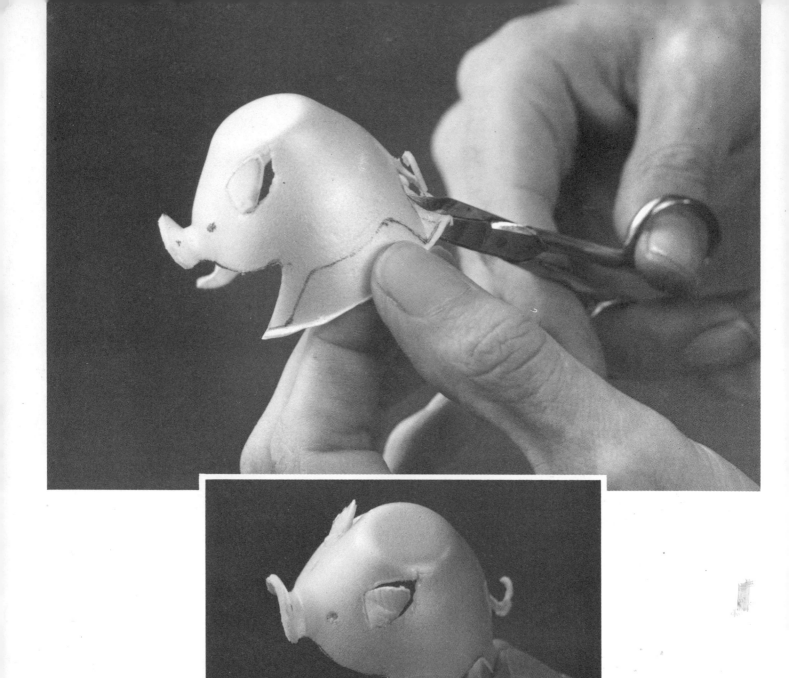

Butterflies

There would not be many butterflies living if this defenceless insect didn't have so many ways to disguise itself from its enemies. Sometimes even we humans think we see only a blossom drifting by on the breeze, or just another flower or leaf, when in fact what we see is a butterfly on the wing or a butterfly at rest. When some butterflies open their wings two large eyes seem to stare out from them. (Insect-eating animals don't like to be stared at.) Other butterflies have the same coloration, yellow and black, as a wasp. Now any animal that has tried to eat a wasp just only once will likely remember the experience and think it a bad idea to try it a second time.

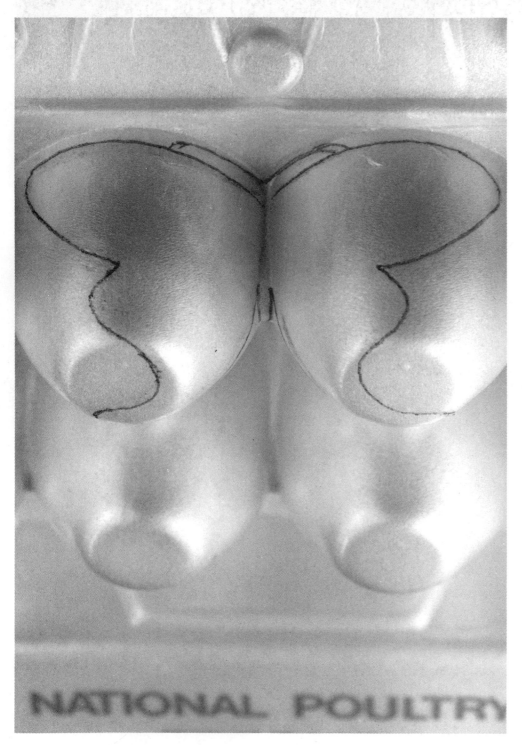

How to make a Butterfly...

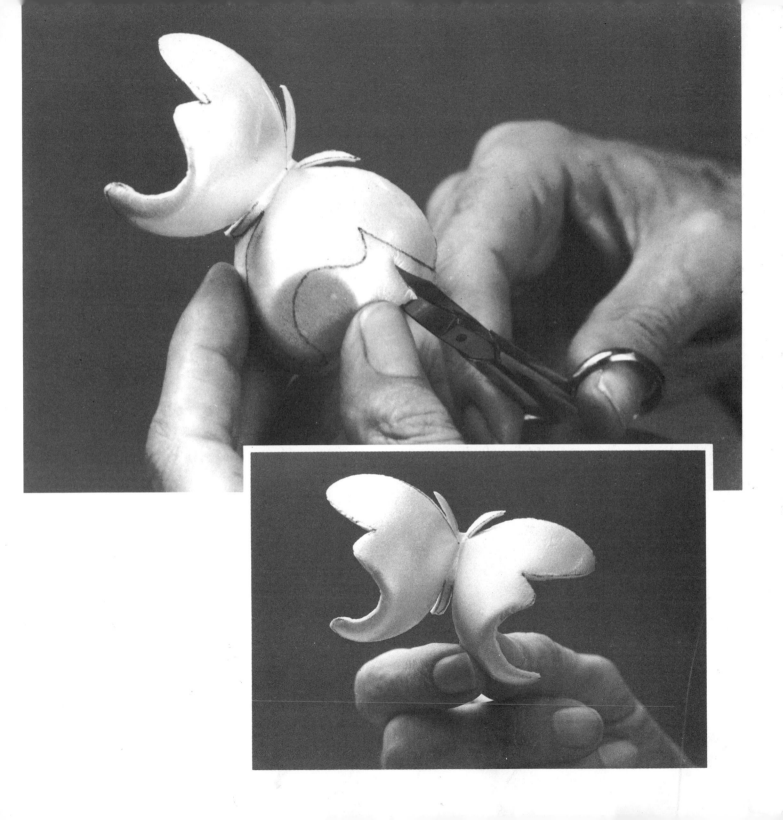

Turtles

There are many different kinds of turtles living in the water, in the desert or on fertile lands around the world.

It is interesting to find out the meanings of the different names given to turtles by the various people where the turtles may be found. *Schildkroete* in German means 'toad with a shield'. *Tortue* in French sounds similar to 'turtle' in English, because both words came from the Roman (Latin) word meaning 'twisted'. Since turtles don't like to live in places with long cold winters, the Eskimo peoples, or Inuit as they call themselves, have no special word for the turtle at all. So when they speak about a turtle they call it *Kilimiguli* which means 'the animal with the thing on top'.

How to make a Turtle....

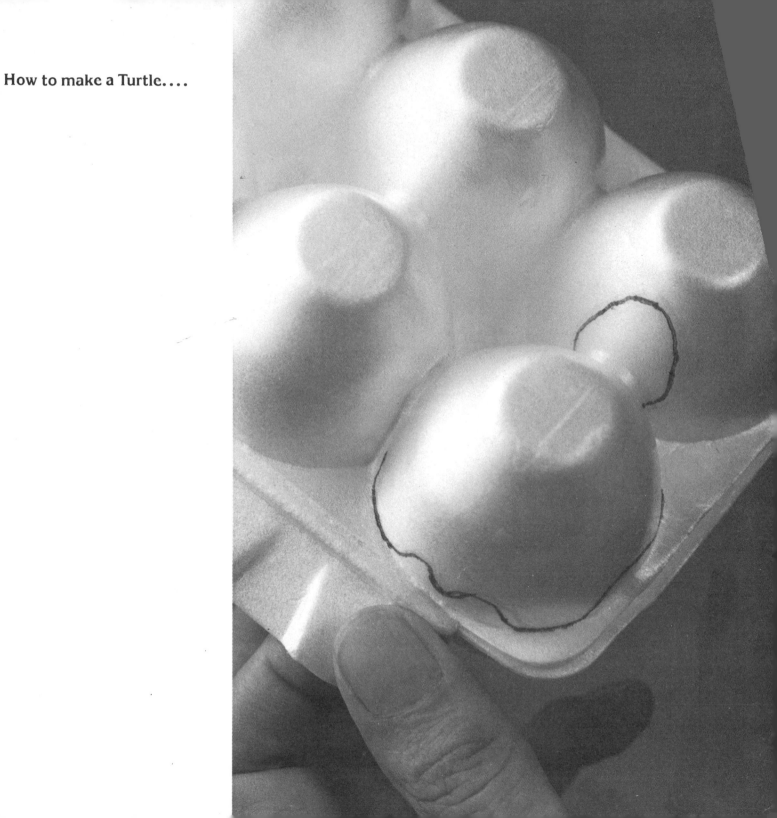

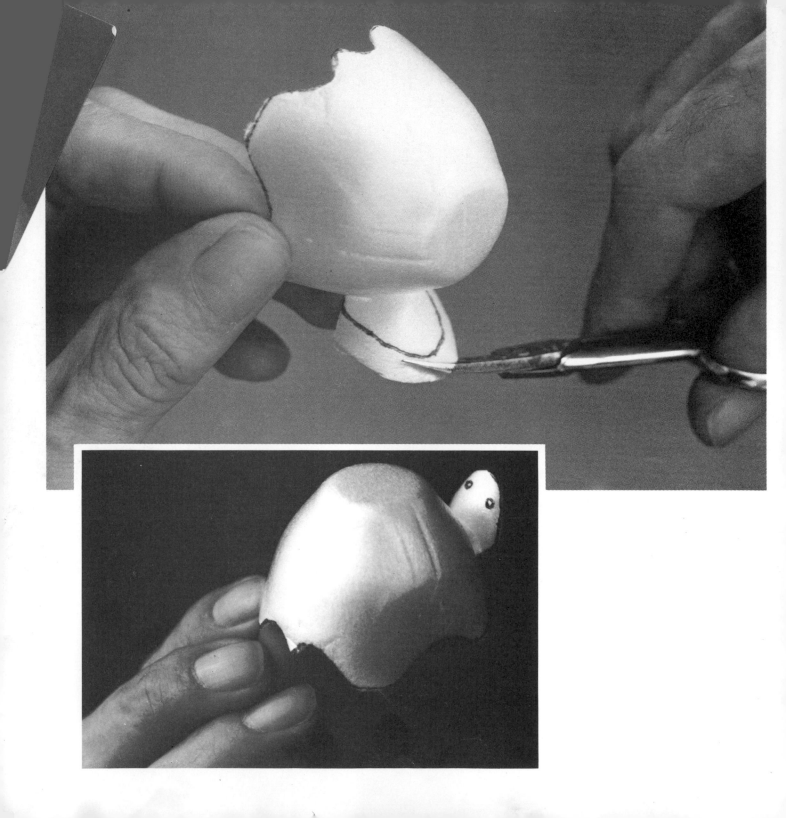

Polar Bear

A true nomad and explorer and once the undisputed ruler of the Far North. An enduring swimmer, diver and wanderer. A survivor of blizzards and cracking ice-floes. Always searching for food and highly protective of their offspring, such are the polar bears.

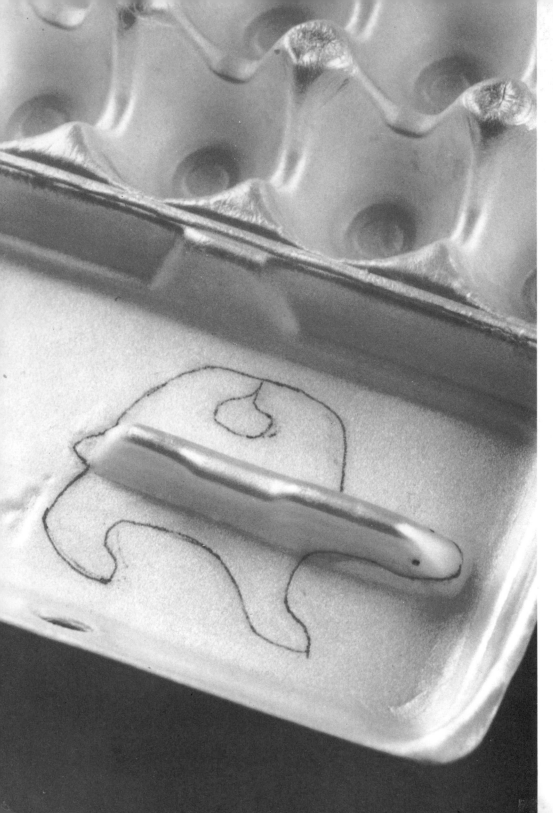

How to make a Polar Bear...

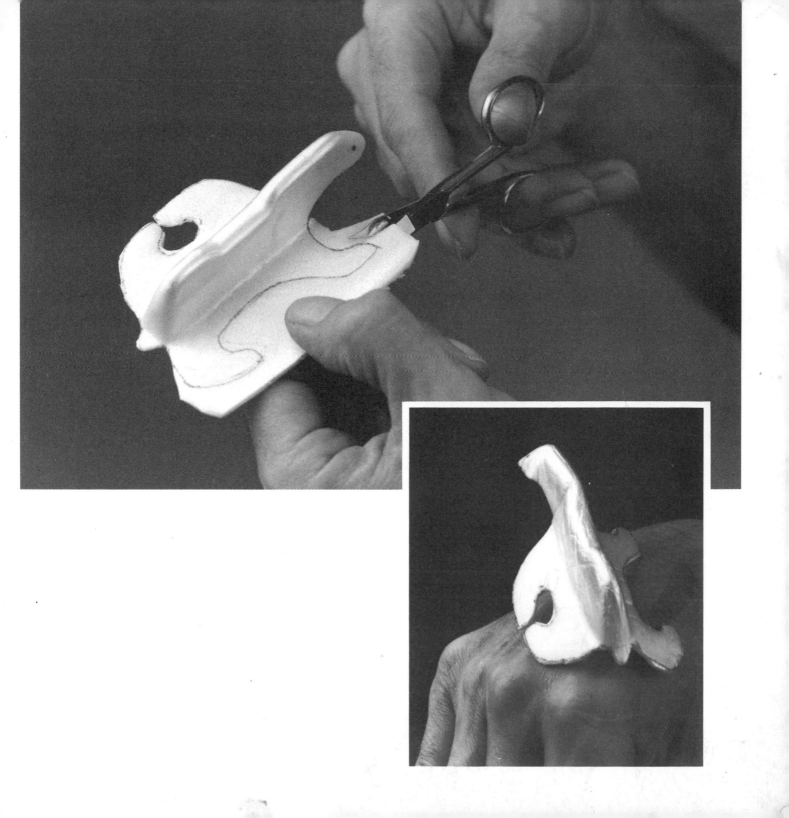

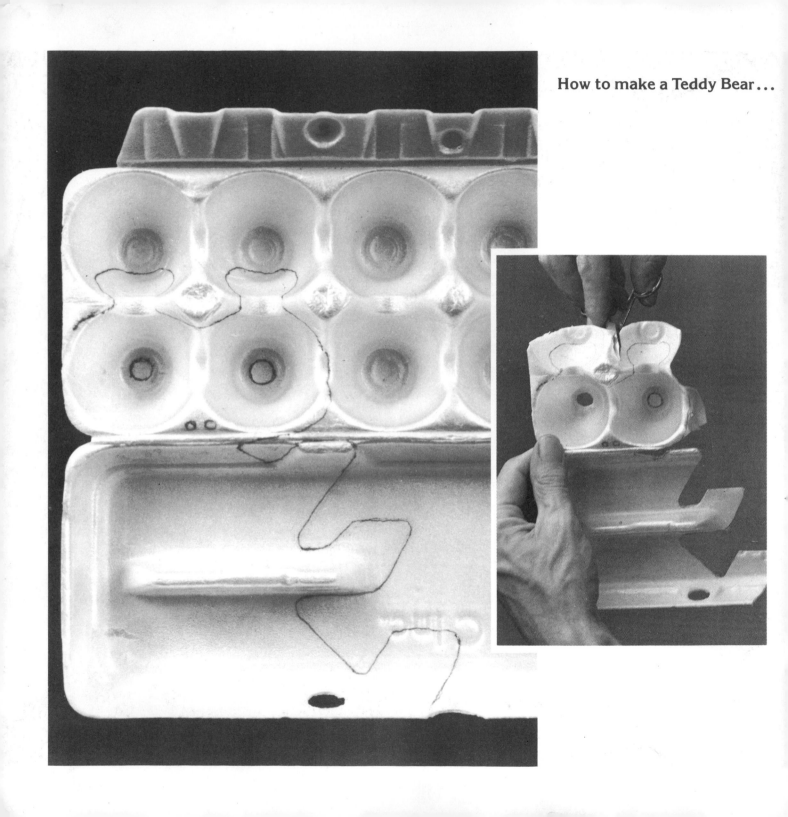

Leopard

When the sun shines through the trees, the shadow on the ground is spotted with patches of light and dark. So is the coat of the leopard, although he is more likely to hunt in the nighttime, since he can see very well in the dark. He glides along silently on his big paws. Any sound is muffled by the soft padding that hides his heavy claws. During the hot daytime he likes to relax, sleep or doze up in the trees, his limbs flopped over the branches like limp sandbags. But he has keen hearing, sight and smell. So if he is hungry and senses that food is walking by in the form of an unsuspecting animal, he can change instantly from a sleeping giant into a spring-loaded jumping machine. He becomes an explosion of strength and attacks with great speed and accurate aim.

How to make a Leopard...

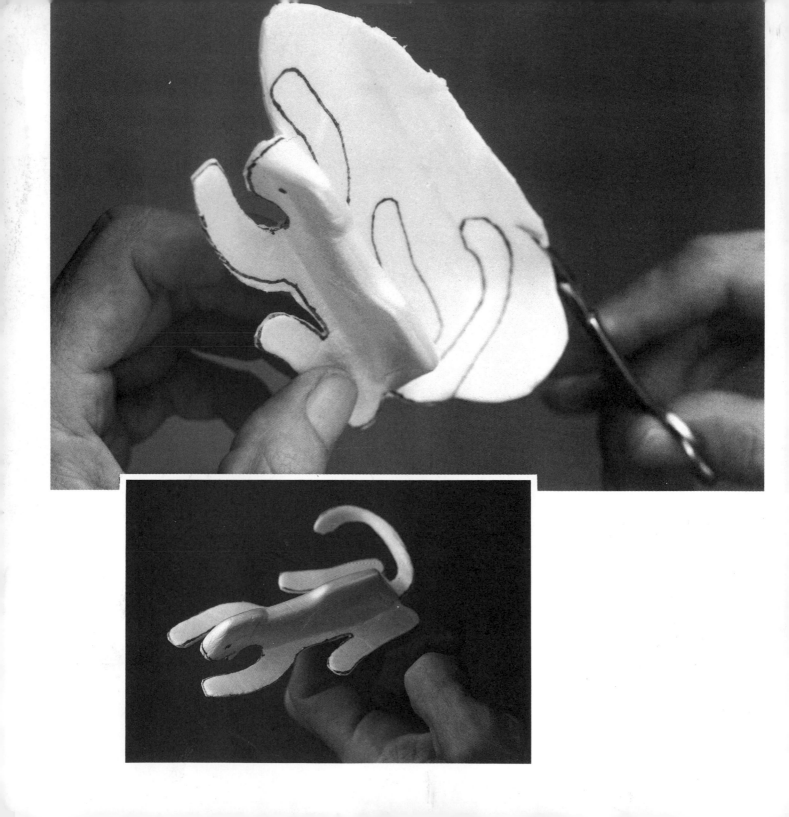

Whales

Whales are impressive in many ways.

Some kinds of whales can grow to the length of three freight-train cars. Yet they are still playful. They stay in touch with each other by long-distance calls, perhaps the oldest long-distance call system in the world. When whales leap out of the water they often land on their backs or their sides. Then what an enormous splash!

When they swim with their humps out of the sea they look like upside-down boats with a hole in the bottom. Whales can spout water out of the blow-holes in their backs up to 30 feet high. Some scientists think this is the way the whales cough. Imagine if one of them had to sneeze....

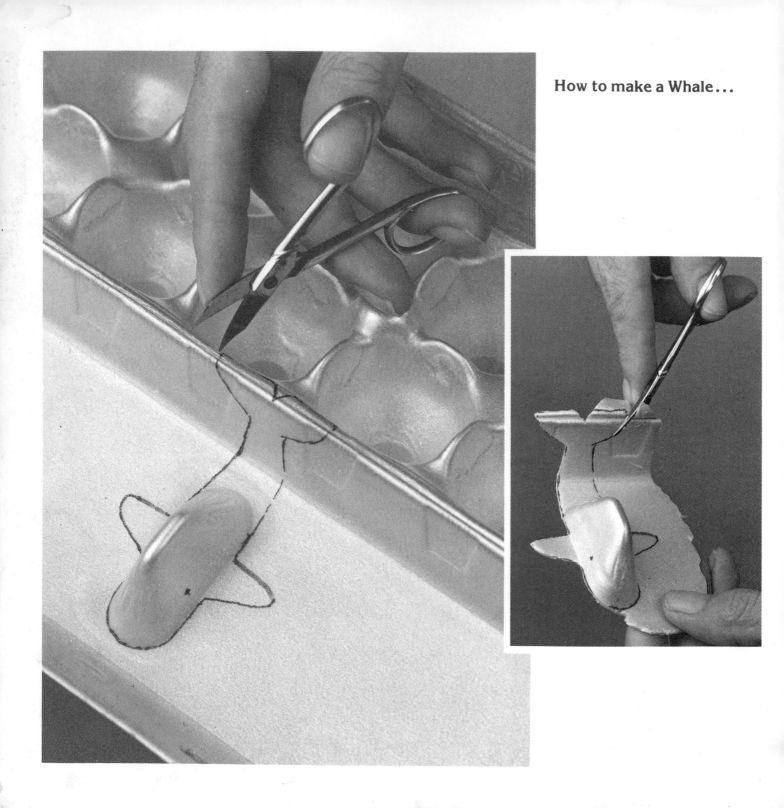

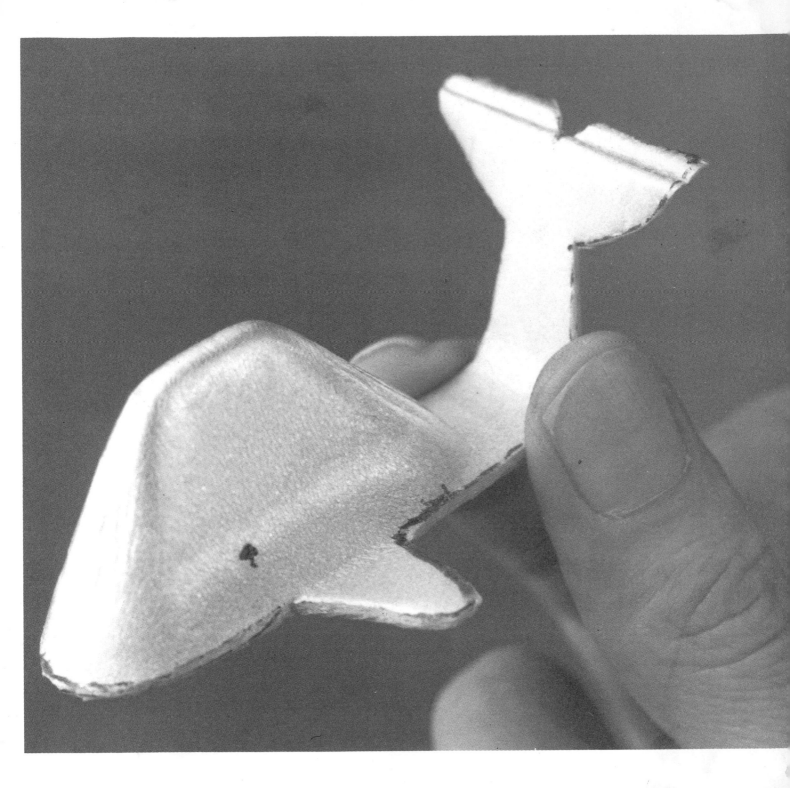

Zebras

Herds of zebras often travel together with other animals, which has advantages for all of them.

When a lion strolls around, birds and monkeys become noisy. The giraffes all face in the same direction, toward the lion. All the other animals will stand at attention. Then the young ones rush towards the centre of their herds and at once all start to run.

The faster gazelles and antelopes tend to get ahead of the other animals and they will notice ahead of time if other lions are waiting in hiding, and swerve aside. For a while all the animals will run in the same direction. As the earth thunders from their hoofs the lion tries to catch up in a cloud of dust.

But the many stripes of the fast-moving zebras can so confuse the lion that all the animals have a chance to get away before the lion has singled out his prey.

The young zebras learn from such experiences that their own safety depends on under-standing and obeying any danger signals from the other animals around them.

How to make a Zebra...

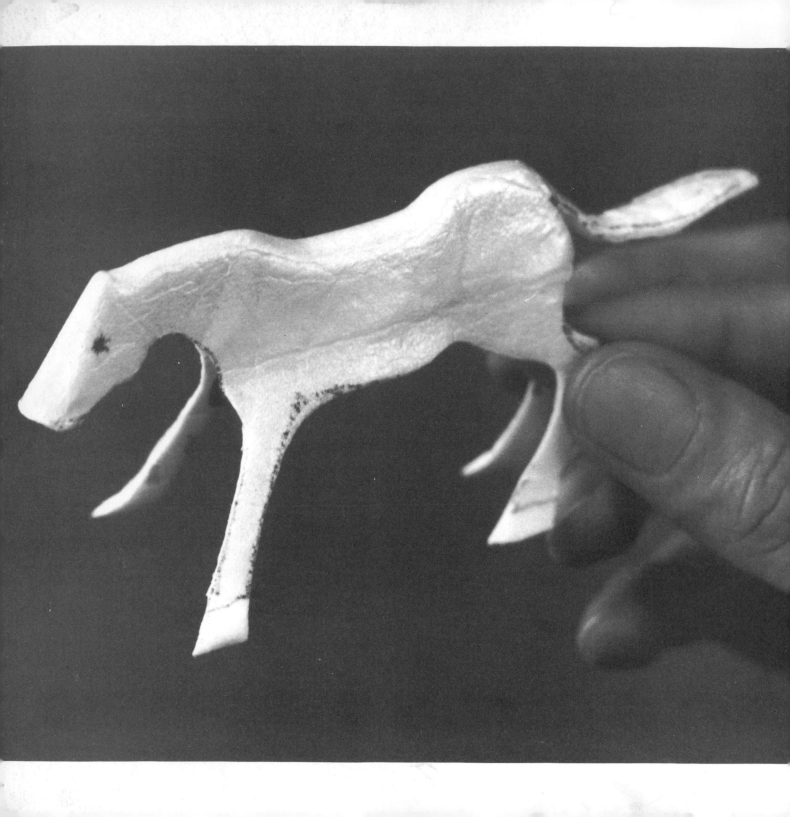

Now let's make some Deer...

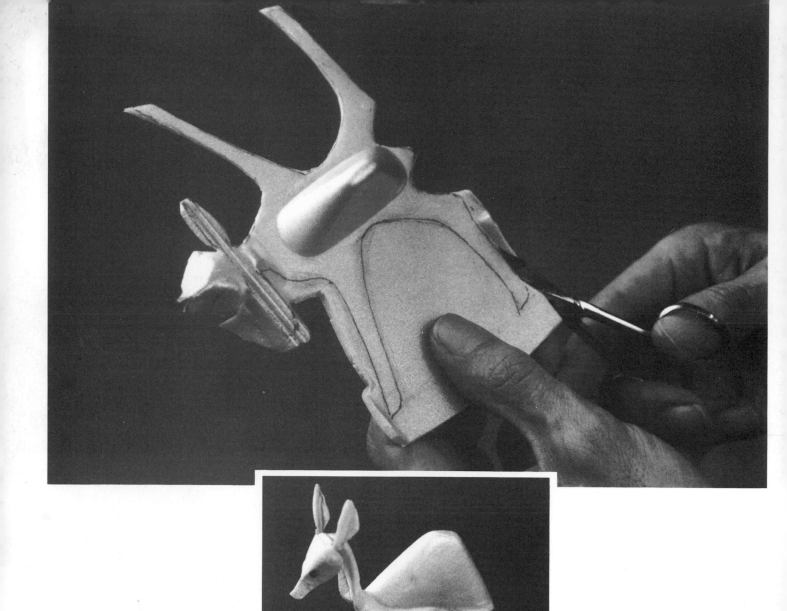

Weasels

Sometimes if we are lucky we can see a weasel move by smoothly like a little wave of drifting snow.

It can also climb trees very fast as it spirals around the trunk to the top. In this way the weasel cannot be easily caught by other predators like owls.

The weasel's gracious looks should not deceive us. The weasel is a fierce, cunning and merciless hunter himself. Since the weasel is said to suck out an egg without even breaking its shell, sneaky people are sometimes called weasels too.

Not only are there many kinds of weasels, but the animal is also called by different names. 'Ermine' is one of the other names we use. The winter coat with its black-tipped tail is worn as a sign of status by people of great importance, like judges and kings.

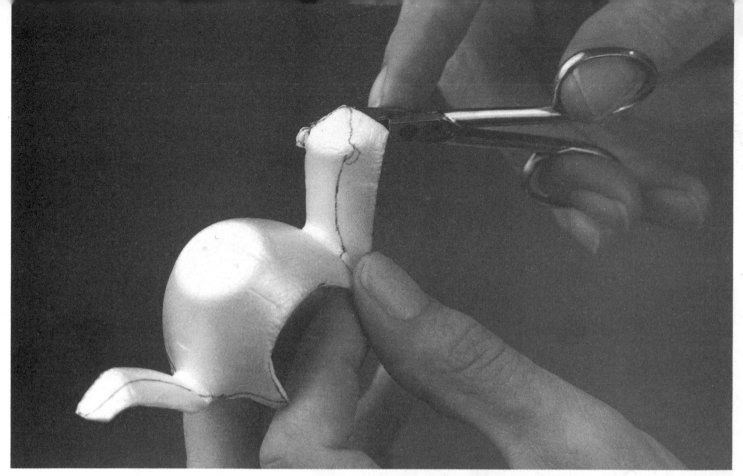

How to make a Weasel...

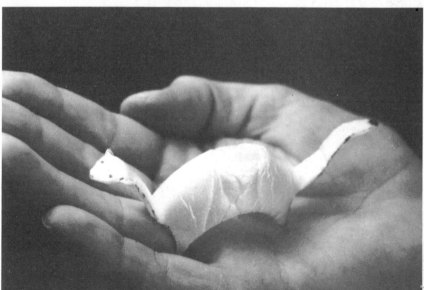

Dogs

People have kept dogs for thousands of years.

So the dog considers himself to be the guardian of his owner's home and belongings. Dogs often understand what we say to them or how we feel better than we can imagine. Since they respect our feelings they make good companions. We too should try to understand their wishes and moods, as expressed by their voices, positions, movements, and other expressions.

Most dogs don't like to share their food with other dogs. They are not like wolves who share their food because they have to go after it together.

How to make a Dog...

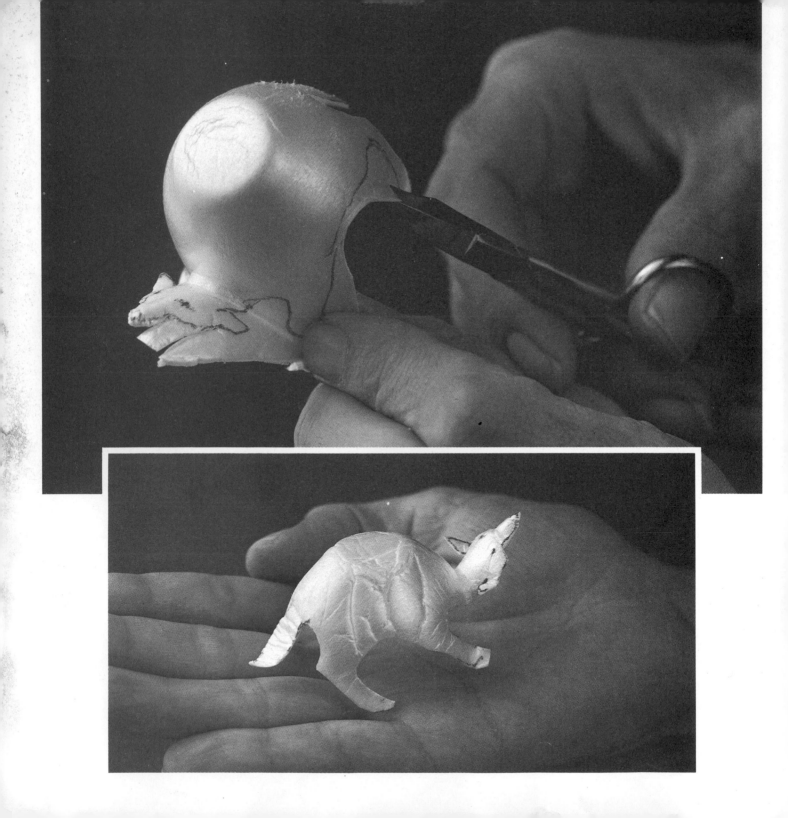

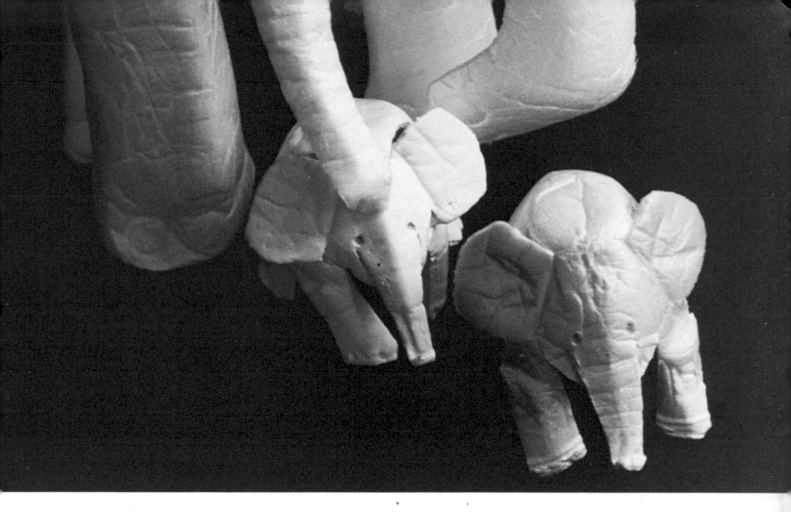

Elephants

Once I watched two young elephants taking a mudbath in an African swamp. As the older ones were slowly moving away, the two young ones kept on wallowing and rolling in the mud. Playfully they pushed each other around and when they were under the muddy water their little trunks stuck out between the water-lilies, like snorkels, to breathe. I did not want to spoil their fun but I was worried about the crocodiles. Finally those two little ones decided to catch up with the rest of the herd and came out of the river plastered with mud which kept them cool. One of the two saw me and pretended he would charge if I didn't go away, lifting his trunk, wiggling his ears and tapping with one leg. But soon he ran after his companion, and then put his trunk on the other one's back.

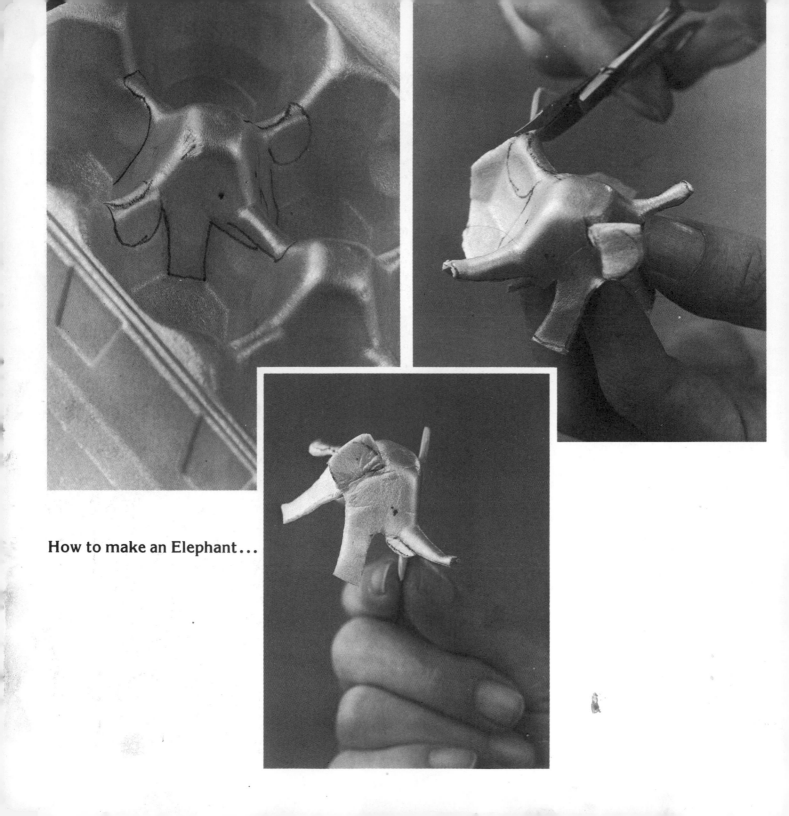

How to make an Elephant...

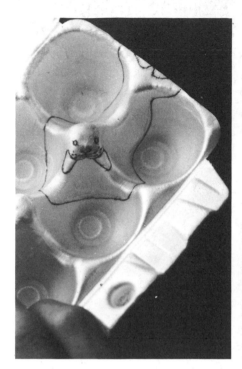

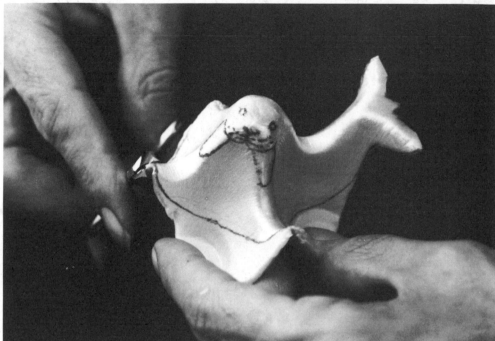

Walrus

This huge animal with his massive flippers, long tusks, drooping moustache and great loud voice is one of the most impressive characters of the Arctic.

How to make a Walrus...

Chameleon

Most precious things are small and so is the lovable chameleon. The chameleon is harmless. It perches on leaves and branches and is almost invisible because it changes colour to match its surroundings. The chameleon is hardly ever seen moving about.

It does not even have to move its head to look around as it can turn one of its popeyes to gaze backwards and the other eye forwards at the same time. So when an insect comes by only its long tongue shoots out to grab the prey and swallow it.

Mice

Housemice have a rather sneaky way of making a living.

They love human places, purely for their own convenience.

Mice belong to the same family of animals as beavers, squirrels and rats. We call them rodents. All rodents have special teeth for nibbling and gnawing, but their tails, besides being different sizes, have different shapes and functions from one animal to another. Because some of these rodents live together with others of their own kind we also call them social animals.

Dinosaurs

There was a time, far back in the past, when Dinosaurs trampled across the land. Some of our ferns grew very tall then, to the size of our trees. And the ancestors of our trees started to grow then, perhaps only as high as grasses. Dinosaurs and other gigantic prehistoric 'monsters' hatched from eggs but some of them grew to be enormous. No matter how big they grew and how sharp their teeth and claws were, we believe they had only very small brains. Nobody knows for sure why all the dinosaurs suddenly disappeared. We only know that once upon a time they ruled the earth and then, quite suddenly, they died out, all around the world. It seems that the climate and the very surface of the earth all changed completely and perhaps although they were so big and strong the dinosaurs did not know how to survive. Other smaller and more adaptable creatures took over and gave rise to the animal kingdom as we know today.

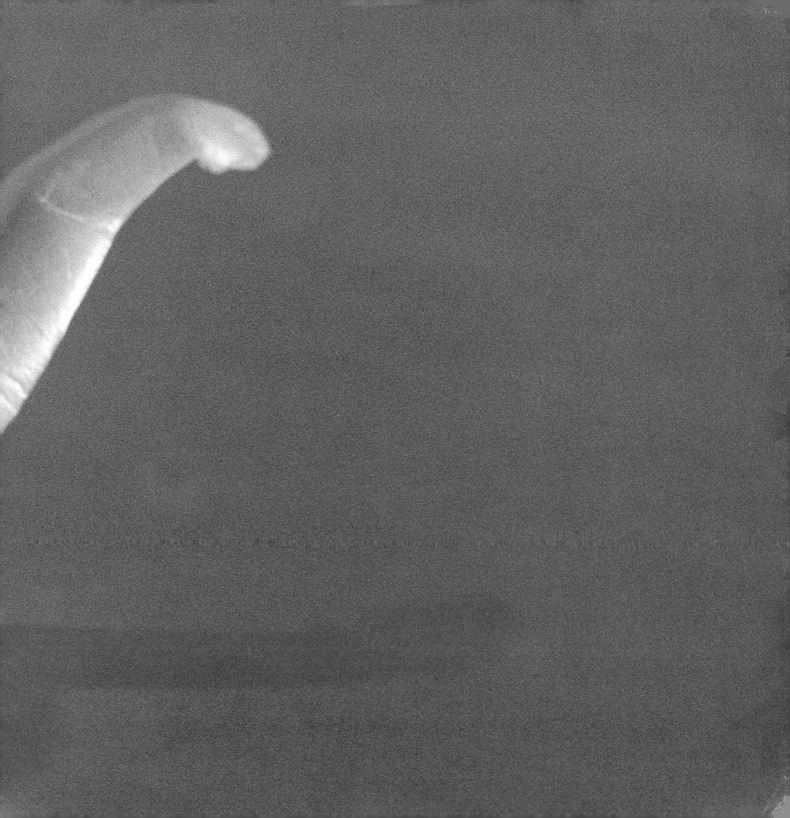

Egg-Carton Zoo

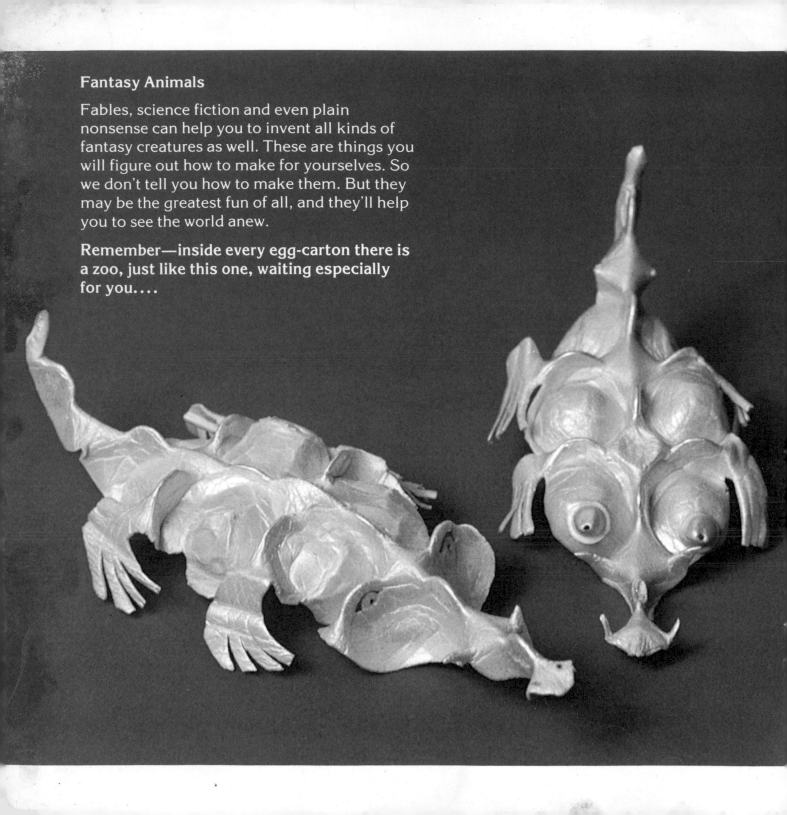

Fantasy Animals

Fables, science fiction and even plain nonsense can help you to invent all kinds of fantasy creatures as well. These are things you will figure out how to make for yourselves. So we don't tell you how to make them. But they may be the greatest fun of all, and they'll help you to see the world anew.

Remember—inside every egg-carton there is a zoo, just like this one, waiting especially for you. . . .